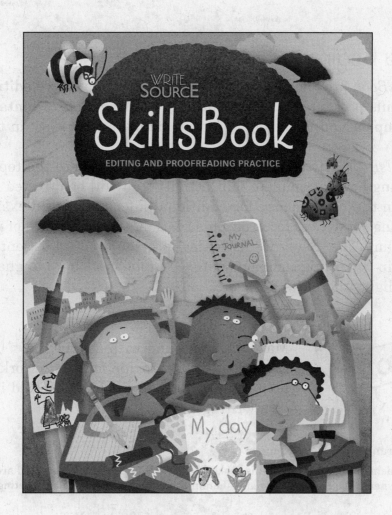

WRITE
SOURCE

SkillsBook

EDITING AND PROOFREADING PRACTICE

MY JOURNAL

My day

. . . a resource of student activities
to accompany *Write Source*

**WRITE SOURCE**®

GREAT SOURCE EDUCATION GROUP
a Houghton Mifflin Company
Wilmington, Massachusetts

# A Few Words About the
# *Write Source SkillsBook*

## Before you begin . . .

The *SkillsBook* provides you with opportunities to practice editing and proofreading skills presented in *Write Source*. The *Write Source* contains guidelines, examples, and models to help you complete your work in the *SkillsBook*.

Each *SkillsBook* activity includes a brief introduction to the topic and examples showing how to complete that activity. You will be directed to the page numbers in the *Write Source* for additional information and examples. The "Proofreading Activities" focus on punctuation, the mechanics of writing, usage, and spelling. The "Sentence Activities" provide practice in sentence combining and in correcting common sentence problems. The "Language Activities" highlight the parts of speech.

Many exercises end with a KEEP GOING activity. Its purpose is to provide follow-up work that will help you apply what you have learned in your own writing.

**Authors:** Pat Sebranek and Dave Kemper

Trademarks and trade names are shown in this book strictly for illustrative purposes and are the property of their respective owners. The authors' references herein should not be regarded as affecting their validity.

Copyright © 2009 by Great Source Education Group, a division of Houghton Mifflin Company. All rights reserved.

Permission is hereby granted to teachers who have purchased the **Write Source Teacher's Resource Package**, grade 2 (ISBN 978-0-669-51838-2), to photocopy in classroom quantities, for use by one teacher and his or her students only, the pages in this work that carry a copyright notice, provided each copy made shows the copyright notice. Such copies may not be sold, and further distribution is expressly prohibited. Teachers who have purchased only the *Write Source SkillsBook* (ISBN 978-0-669-01623-9) may not reproduce or transmit this work or portions thereof in any other form or by any other electronic or mechanical means, including any information storage or retrieval system, unless expressly permitted by federal copyright law or authorized in writing by Great Source Education Group. Address inquiries to Permissions, Great Source Education Group, 181 Ballardvale Street, Wilmington, MA 01887.

**Great Source** and **Write Source** are registered trademarks of Houghton Mifflin Company.

Printed in the United States of America

International Standard Book Number: 978-0-669-01623-9 (student edition)

6 7 8 9 10 -1429- 15 14 13 12

International Standard Book Number: 978-0-669-01624-6 (teacher's edition)

1 2 3 4 5 6 7 8 9 10 -1429- 15 14 13 12 11 10 09 08
4500359951

# Table of Contents

**Proofreading Activities**

## Using Punctuation

## Checking Mechanics

## Using the Right Word

## Sentence Activities

## Language Activities

### Nouns

### Pronouns

### Verbs

### Adjectives

### Other Parts of Speech

### Parts of Speech Review

# Proofreading Activities

The activities in this section include sentences that need to be checked for punctuation, mechanics, or usage. Most of the activities also include helpful *Write Source* references. In addition, KEEP GOING, which is at the end of many activities, encourages follow-up practice of certain skills.

*Name*
_____

# Periods as End Punctuation

A **period** is used as a signal to stop at the end of a sentence. Put a period at the end of a telling sentence.

 **Put periods at the ends of these telling sentences.**

**1.** Our class lines up at the main door ____•____

**2.** Sometimes we make our teacher smile _____

**3.** We play indoors on rainy days _____

**4.** There are some great new books in the library _____

**5.** I like to write funny stories _____

**B** **Write two telling sentences about your school.**

**1.** _____

_____

**2.** _____

_____

© Great Source. All rights reserved.

**C** **Put a period at the end of each sentence in this letter.**

October 10, 2006

Dear Aunt Fran,

I like school this year There are 22 kids in my class A new boy sits next to me His name is Robert I think we're going to be friends I'll let you know in my next letter

Love,

Timmy

**Now answer these questions about the letter.**

**1.** How many telling sentences are in the letter? _____

**2.** How many periods are in the letter? _____

© Great Source. All rights reserved.

Name _____

# Periods After Abbreviations

Use **periods** after these abbreviations:
Mr., Mrs., Ms., and Dr.

Dr. Green    Mrs. Linn

(**Dr.** is the abbreviation for **doctor**.)

**A** Put periods after the abbreviations in these sentences. (Some sentences need more than one period.)

**1.** Mrs. Linn is our teacher.

**2.** Mr and Mrs Linn have three rabbits.

**3.** Mr Linn gave the rabbits their names.

**4.** They are Ms Hop, Mr Skip, and Mrs Jump.

**5.** Mrs Linn took the rabbits to Dr Green for shots.

**6.** Dr Green said, "Those are good names!"

**7.** Mrs Linn told Dr Green that Mr Linn made up

the names.

© Great Source. All rights reserved.

**B** Write two names for rabbits. One name should start with Mr. and one with Mrs. Then write two sentences that use the names.

Name: _Mr._____

Name: _Mrs._____

1. _____

_____

_____

2. _____

_____

_____

**C** Write the names of four grown-ups. Be sure to write Mr., Mrs., Ms., or Dr. before each name.

1. _____

2. _____

3. _____

4. _____

© Great Source. All rights reserved.

Name _____

# Question Marks

Put a **question mark** after a sentence that asks a question.

What is the longest river?

 Put a question mark after each sentence that asks a question. Put a period after each of the other sentences.

**1.** The world's longest river is the Nile _____

**2.** Where is the Nile _____

**3.** The Nile River is in Africa _____

**4.** Are there crocodiles in the Nile _____

**5.** You could jump in and find out _____

**6.** Are you kidding _____

**7.** I'd rather just ask someone _____

**8.** Are you afraid of crocodiles _____

**9.** Who wouldn't be afraid _____

© Great Source. All rights reserved.

8

B

**Put a period or a question mark at the end of each sentence in this paragraph.**

Lots of animals live in rivers Of course, fish live in rivers What else lives in rivers Snails, frogs, and turtles live in and around rivers Have you heard of river otters They are very good at diving They can stay underwater for four minutes Do you know any other animals that live in rivers

**Write two questions about rivers. Remember to use question marks!**

1. _____

_____

2. _____

_____

© Great Source. All rights reserved.

Name _____

# Exclamation Points

Put an **exclamation point** after an *excited* word. Also put an exclamation point after a sentence showing strong feeling.

Help! ←        Yikes!

Don't touch that! ←

 **Use an exclamation point or period to finish each sentence. Remember, an exclamation point is used after each *excited* word and after each sentence that shows strong feeling. Telling sentences need a period.**

**1.** I found a treasure map___!___

**2.** It was in my closet_____

**3.** I found the map when I cleaned my room_____

**4.** Wow_____

**5.** Let's find the treasure_____

**6.** We should ask our parents before we look_____

**7.** This could be fun_____

© Great Source. All rights reserved.

**B** Each of the following sentences needs an exclamation point or a question mark. Put the correct end punctuation after each sentence.

**1.** Look, Tom, it's a cave _____

**2.** It's dark _____

**3.** It's creepy _____

**4.** Did you see that _____

**5.** What is it _____

**6.** It's a bat _____

**7.** Wow, that's neat _____

**8.** Here we go _____

Imagine that you are in a dark cave. Write a sentence that ends with an exclamation point.

_____

_____

© Great Source. All rights reserved.

Name _____

# End Punctuation

Use a **period (.)** after a telling sentence. Use a **question mark (?)** after a sentence that asks a question. Use an **exclamation point (!)** after a sentence that shows strong feeling.

 **Put the correct end punctuation after each sentence.**

**1.** Dad's taking us to the zoo __!__

**2.** Hooray!  Let's have a race to the car _____

**3.** What animal does Dad like _____

**4.** He likes the elephants _____

**5.** What do you think Mom wants to see _____

**6.** She'll probably watch the giraffes _____

**7.** What should we do _____

**8.** Let's go see the seals _____

© Great Source.  All rights reserved.

12

**B** Write a telling sentence, an asking sentence, and a sentence showing strong feeling about your favorite dinner.

Telling Sentence: _____

_____

Asking Sentence: _____

_____

Strong Feeling Sentence: _____

_____

**C** Ask a partner a question. Write your partner's name, the question you asked, and your partner's answer.

Partner's Name: _____

Question: _____

_____

Answer: _____

_____

© Great Source. All rights reserved.

13

Name _____

# End Punctuation Review

Use a **period** after a telling sentence. Use a **question mark** after a sentence that asks a question. Use an **exclamation point** after a sentence that shows strong feeling.

 **Put the correct end punctuation after each sentence.**

Does this ever happen to you It's time for

bed, but you're not sleepy You try to lie still

You look around You just have to get up You

want to get a book or a toy You try to be

quiet It's hard to see in the dark You make a

loud noise Someone says, "What's going on in

there" Then you hear, "Get back in bed"

© Great Source. All rights reserved.

14

**B** Draw a picture of something you like to do after school.

**C** Write three sentences about your picture. First write a telling sentence. Next write a question. Then write a sentence that shows strong feeling.

**1.** Telling Sentence:_____

_____

**2.** Asking Sentence:_____

_____

**3.** Strong Feeling Sentence:_____

_____

© Great Source. All rights reserved.

Name _____

# Commas Between Words in a Series

Put **commas** between words in a series.

The five senses are sight, hearing, taste, smell, and touch.

 **A** **Put commas where they are needed in these sentences.**

**1.** Most foods taste sweet, sour, or salty.

**2.** Smell sight and taste help us enjoy food.

**3.** Almost everybody likes warm bread biscuits and dinner rolls.

**4.** Lilies lilacs and roses smell good.

**5.** Cats can see only black white and gray.

**6.** Dogs cats and bats hear all kinds of sounds.

**7.** Sounds can be loud soft or just right.

**8.** Teddy bears are soft cuddly and fuzzy.

© Great Source. All rights reserved.

16

**B**  **List three or four things in each category below.**

| My Favorite **Tastes** | My Favorite **Smells** | My Favorite **Sounds** |
|---|---|---|
|  |  |  |
|  |  |  |
|  |  |  |
|  |  |  |

**C**  **Finish the sentences below using words from your lists. Remember to use commas between words in a series.**

**1.** My favorite tastes are _____

_____ and _____ .

**2.** My favorite smells are _____

_____ and _____ .

**3.** My favorite sounds are _____

_____ and _____ .

© Great Source. All rights reserved.

Name

_____

# Commas in Compound Sentences

A **compound sentence** is two short sentences connected by *or*, *and*, or *but*. Always use a **comma** before the connecting word.

I have a goldfish, and I feed it once a day.

 **A** Add a comma to each of these compound sentences.

**1.** I love hamburgers, but I do not like onions.

**2.** My brother is three and he goes to preschool.

**3.** You can walk or you can ride your bike.

**4.** Dad came to the concert but Mom had to work.

**5.** Our teacher is nice and she loves dogs.

**6.** Sara will play the piano or she will sing.

**7.** I asked Lee to play ball but he was busy.

© Great Source.  All rights reserved.

18

**Write compound sentences using the pairs of sentences below. Use the connecting word in parentheses to complete each sentence. Remember to add commas!**

Do you see the bees? Can you hear them? (or)
**Do you see the bees, or can you hear them?**

**1.** Bees are busy. They all have jobs to do. *(and)*

_____

_____

_____

**2.** Most bees work. The queen bee does not work. *(but)*

_____

_____

_____

**3.** Bees care for the queen. They make honey. *(or)*

_____

_____

_____

© Great Source. All rights reserved.

Name _____

# Commas to Set Off a Speaker's Words

When you write a speaker's exact words, you may tell who is speaking at the **beginning** of the sentence, or at the **end** of the sentence. Use a comma to set off the speaker's words, as shown below.

Mr. Kent said, "Kari, you may begin your report."

"My report is on birds," Kari said.

**A** Put commas where they are needed in these sentences.

"Many birds migrate in the winter," Kari said.

Darrin asked "What does *migrate* mean?"

"Migrate means that some birds go to a new place in winter" Kari answered. She added "Birds migrate to find food and water."

"That's very interesting" said Mr. Kent.

© Great Source. All rights reserved.

**B** **Write questions that Bill and Regina might ask about birds and migration. Use question marks and commas correctly.**

Bill asked __" _____

_____

_____ "

Regina asked __" _____

_____

_____ "

**List three places you would like to migrate (travel) to.**

1. _____

2. _____

3. _____

© Great Source. All rights reserved.

*Name* _____

# Comma Between a City and a State

Put a **comma** between the name of a city and a state.

Austin, Texas        Salem, Oregon

 **A** **Put commas between the cities and states below.**

**1.** Calumet Michigan        **4.** Portland   Maine

**2.** Casper   Wyoming        **5.** Dallas   Texas

**3.** Williamsburg   Virginia        **6.** Dayton   Ohio

 **B** **Write the name of the city and state shown on page 408 in your *Write Source*. Then write the name of another city and its state. Put a comma between the city and state.**

**1.** _____

**2.** _____

© Great Source. All rights reserved.

22

**Draw a picture of a place in your city or town. Beneath your drawing, write sentences about your picture.**

I live in_____

_____

_____

_____

© Great Source. All rights reserved.

*Name* _____

# Comma Between the Day and the Year

Put a **comma** between the day and the year.

January 17, 2009

November 12, 2009

**October 2009**

| S | M | T | W | T | F | S |
|---|---|---|---|---|---|---|
|   |   |   |   | 1 | 2 | 3 |
| 4 | 5 | 6 | 7 | 8 | 9 | 10 |
| 11 | 12 | 13 | 14 | 15 | 16 | 17 |
| 18 | 19 | 20 | 21 | 22 | 23 | 24 |
| 25 | 26 | 27 | 28 | 29 | 30 | 31 |

**A** Look at the calendar on this page. Then write the correct month, day, and year.

**1.** Write the date that is circled.

October 11, 2009

**2.** Write the date that has a diamond around it.

_____

**3.** Write the date for the last day of the month.

_____

**4.** Write the date for the first Monday of the month.

_____

© Great Source. All rights reserved.

**B** Write the dates for the following days. Be sure to include the month, day, and year. The months are listed on page 426 in *Write Source*.

**1.** Your next birthday:

_____

**2.** Today:

_____

**3.** Tomorrow:

_____

Write a true or make-believe sentence about the day you were born. Include the date of your birth in your sentence.

_____

_____

_____

_____

   © Great Source. All rights reserved.

*Name* _____

# Commas in Letters

Put **commas** after the greeting and the closing of a letter.

Dear Grandpa Joe, ← **greeting**
    I love my new fishing rod! Thank you!
Can we go fishing soon? I hope so!
      Love,
      Ben ↖ **closing**

**A**   **Put commas where they belong in these letters.**

November 10, 2009
Dear Ben
    Ask your mom when your family is coming to Florida. Then we can go fishing.
      Love
      Grandpa Joe

November 18, 2009
Dear Grandpa Joe
    We are coming to see you on December 23. I can't wait! My tackle box is ready.
      Love
      Ben

© Great Source. All rights reserved.

**B** Put commas in Grandpa's letter. Then pretend you are Ben. Write what you would say in your next letter to Grandpa Joe. Be sure to put commas in the right places.

---

November 24, 2009

Dear Ben

    I will be seeing you in one month! We'll camp out in a tent. We'll have a campfire.

        Love

        Grandpa Joe

---

_____
(Date)

_____
(Greeting)

_____

_____

_____
(Closing)

_____
(Signature)

© Great Source. All rights reserved.

Name _____

# Comma Review

This activity reviews comma uses you have learned.

 **Put a comma between the names of the cities and the states in these sentences.**

**1.** You can see mountains from Portland⌃Oregon.

**2.** The James River goes through Richmond Virginia.

**3.** El Paso Texas, is near Mexico.

**4.** Sitka Alaska, is on the Pacific Ocean.

**5.** Hilo Hawaii, is part of an island.

 **Put a comma between the day and the year in these sentences.**

**1.** George Washington was born February 22 1732.

**2.** The first nickel was made on May 16 1866.

**3.** On February 7 1867, Laura Ingalls Wilder was born.

**4.** The astronaut Sally Ride was born May 26 1951.

© Great Source. All rights reserved.

## C Put commas between words in a series in these sentences.

**1.** Red orange yellow and green are rainbow colors.

**2.** My uncle aunt and cousin live in Michigan.

**3.** Jonathan likes snowboarding sledding and skiing.

**4.** My family has two cats one dog and a turtle.

**5.** I send letters notes and e-mail messages.

## D Put commas where they are needed.

Maggie asked "What kind of seashell is that?"

"It's a heart cockle" Molly said. "If you put two together, they form a heart."

"Amazing!" Maggie added. "What's this one?"

"It's called a turkey wing" Molly answered.

"That's a perfect name! It looks just like one" said Maggie.

© Great Source. All rights reserved.

Name _____

# Making Contractions 1

A **contraction** turns two words into one word. To make a contraction, put an **apostrophe** where one or more letters are left out.

| Two Words | Contraction |
|-----------|-------------|
| does not | doesn't |
| we have | we've |

**A** In the second column, cross out the letters that are left out of the contraction in the first column.

| Contraction | Two Words |
|-------------|-----------|
| **1.** I'm | I am |
| **2.** she'll | she will |
| **3.** he's | he is |
| **4.** they're | they are |
| **5.** he'd | he would |
| **6.** hasn't | has not |
| **7.** we'll | we will |
| **8.** shouldn't | should not |

© Great Source. All rights reserved.

30

**Make contractions from the words below. Remember to use an apostrophe each time!**

**1.** do not _____

**2.** that is _____

**3.** cannot _____

**4.** I have _____

**On each blank below, write the contraction for the words in parentheses.**

**1.** _____ going to make a mask.
(I am)

**2.** _____ make it out of a paper bag.
(I will)

**3.** _____ going to be a scary mask.
(It is)

**4.** Dad _____ know I am making it.
(does not)

© Great Source. All rights reserved.

*Name*

# Making Contractions 2

A **contraction** turns two words into one word. To make a contraction, put an **apostrophe** where one or more letters are left out.

| Two Words | Contraction |
|-----------|-------------|
| she will  | she'll      |

**A** In each sentence, underline the contraction. Then write the word or words the contraction stands for.

1. "Peter <u>didn't</u> obey Mom," said Flopsy.  did not

2. "You can't go to the ball," she told Cinderella.

   _____

3. "You wouldn't help me," said the Little Red Hen.

   _____

4. "I couldn't sleep in that bumpy bed," said the princess.

   _____

5. The wolf said, "I'll blow your house down." _____

6. "I'm a real boy!" shouted Pinocchio. _____

© Great Source. All rights reserved.

**B** Write the two words that each contraction stands for.

1. doesn't _____

2. hasn't _____

3. he's _____

4. I've _____

5. isn't _____

6. it's _____

7. we're _____

8. you'll _____

Write a sentence using one of the contractions above.

_____

_____

_____

© Great Source.  All rights reserved.

*Name* _____

# Apostrophes to Show Ownership

Add an **apostrophe** and an *s* to a word to show ownership.

Tom has a boat.     It is Tom's boat.

**A**   Each phrase below shows ownership. Draw a picture in each box.

| | |
|---|---|
| the cat's rug | the bird's nest |
| Susan's jump rope | my mother's hat |

© Great Source. All rights reserved.

**B** Write the words below to show ownership. Be sure to add an apostrophe and an *s* to each word.

**1.** the _____ leaves
   (tree)

**2.** the _____ string
   (kite)

**3.** the _____ wing
   (airplane)

**4.** the _____ tail
   (bird)

**C** Write the names below to show ownership. Add an apostrophe and an *s* to each name.

**1.** I see _____ purple pencil.
   (Maria)

**2.** This is _____ math book.
   (Don)

**3.** _____ backpack is heavier than mine.
   (Jane)

**4.** _____ idea notebook is on the desk.
   (Sol)

© Great Source. All rights reserved.

Name _____

# Underlining Titles

**Underline** the titles of books and magazines.

     **a book** — <u>Onion Sundaes</u>

     **a magazine** — <u>3, 2, 1 Contact</u>

 **A**    **Underline the titles in the following sentences.**

**1.** My sister's favorite book is <u>Pocahontas</u>.

**2.** My grandmother has a book called <u>Mrs. Bird</u>.

**3.** <u>Kids Discover</u> is a magazine for kids.

**4.** The title of our book is <u>Write Source</u>.

**5.** <u>Ranger Rick</u> is a nature magazine for kids.

**6.** I just read <u>Ira Sleeps Over</u> by Bernard Waber.

**7.** My dad reads <u>National Geographic</u> every month.

**8.** Our teacher is reading <u>All About Sam</u> to us.

© Great Source. All rights reserved.

**B** Complete the following sentences. Remember to underline the titles.

**1.** My favorite book is _____

_____ .

**2.** My favorite magazine is _____

_____ .

**3.** The title of the last book I read is _____

_____ .

Draw a cover for one of your favorite books. Write the book title on your cover.

© Great Source.  All rights reserved.

Name _____

# Quotation Marks Before and After a Speaker's Words

Comic strips make it easy to tell who is speaking. They use speech balloons. Here Mom and Steve are talking about dinner.

When you write sentences, you use **quotation marks** to show the speaker's exact words.

Steve asked, "Mom, may we make pizza for dinner?"

"That sounds really good to me," Mom said.

© Great Source. All rights reserved.

38

**A** **Read the speech balloons. Then write the sentences below. Put quotation marks where they are needed.**

May we make pepperoni pizza?

Yes, Let's add something else.

Steve asked,_____

_____

Mom answered,_____

_____

How about mushrooms?

Great choice!

Steve asked,_____

_____

Mom said,_____

_____

© Great Source. All rights reserved.

*Name* _____

# Punctuation Review

This review covers punctuation marks you have learned.

 **A** **Fill in each list below.**

| Cat Names | City Names | Food Names |
|---|---|---|
| 1. Buddy | 1. _____ | 1. _____ |
| 2. _____ | 2. _____ | 2. _____ |
| 3. _____ | 3. _____ | 3. _____ |

**B** **Use your lists to write sentences.**

**1.** Write a **telling sentence** about three cats.

_____

_____

**2.** Write an **asking sentence** about three cities.

_____

_____

© Great Source. All rights reserved.

**3.** Write an **exciting sentence** about three foods.

_____

_____

**C**  **Write contractions for the words below.**

**1.** did not _____   **6.** cannot _____

**2.** you are _____   **7.** we have _____

**3.** I am _____   **8.** has not _____

**4.** it is _____   **9.** is not _____

**5.** they will_____   **10.** she is _____

**D**  **Fill in each blank with a word that shows ownership.**

**1.** The dog has a ball. It is the _____ ball.

**2.** Alisha has a computer. It is _____ computer.

**3.** Our teacher has a bike. It is our _____ bike.

**4.** Barry has a pet bird. It is _____ pet bird.

© Great Source. All rights reserved.
© Great Source. All rights reserved.

Name
_____

# Capital Letters for Names and Titles

Use **capital letters** for people's names and titles.

**title**     **name**

Mr. Thomas lives in a little house.
Mrs. Thomas lives there, too.

**Add capital letters where they are needed. Cross out the lower-case letter you want to change. Write the correct capital letter above it.**

                M   C

**1.** Our class helper is m̷rs. ȼantu.

**2.** The school nurse is mr. thomas.

**3.** Yesterday, will and I went to see dr. paula.

**4.** I asked ms. demarko to read me a story.

**5.** Mr. and mrs. chang picked us up at camp.

**6.** Tomorrow, ms. banks and sally are coming over.

**7.** Our dentist is dr. villa.

© Great Source. All rights reserved.

42

**B** Draw a picture or paste a photo of your favorite grown-up.

Write two sentences telling why you like this grown-up. Make sure to use the grown-up's title and name each time.

1. _____

_____

2. _____

_____

© Great Source. All rights reserved.

Name _____

# Capital Letters for Days of the Week

Use **capital letters** for days of the week.

S̲unday        W̲ednesday

 **A** **Answer the questions below. Remember to use capital letters correctly.**

**1.** Which day comes after Saturday? _____Sunday_____

**2.** Which day is between Tuesday and Thursday?

_____

**3.** Which day begins with the letter "F"? _____

**4.** Which day is the first day of the school week?

_____

**5.** Which day comes after Friday? _____

**6.** Which day is before Wednesday? _____

**7.** Which day comes before Friday? _____

© Great Source. All rights reserved.

44

**B** Put the days of the week in the correct order, starting with Sunday.

Thursday    Sunday    Tuesday    Monday

Friday    Wednesday    Saturday

1. _____

2. _____

3. _____

4. _____

5. _____

6. _____

7. _____

Write a sentence about your favorite day of the week.

_____

_____

_____

© Great Source. All rights reserved.

Name _____

# Capital Letters for Months of the Year 1

Use **capital letters** for the months of the year.

February    May

**A** Use capital letters for the months in these sentences.

                                M
1. The first day of spring is in march.

2. The first day of summer is in june.

3. The first day of fall is in september.

4. The first day of winter is in december.

5. The first month of the year is january.

6. The shortest month is february.

7. Usually july and august are the hottest months.

8. april showers bring spring flowers.

© Great Source. All rights reserved.

**B** Here are three more months. Write each month correctly.

may _____

october _____

november _____

Write one sentence about each month above.

1. _____

_____

_____

2. _____

_____

_____

3. _____

_____

_____

© Great Source. All rights reserved.

*Name*

# Capital Letters for Months of the Year 2

Use **capital letters** for the months of the year.

**A** Read the sentences below. Write the month correctly on the line after each sentence.

**1.** Handwriting Day is the 12th of january. _January_

**2.** Groundhog Day is in february. _____

**3.** Arbor Day is in april. _____

**4.** Memorial Day is the last Monday in may. _____

**5.** My birthday is in june. _____

**6.** Independence Day is the fourth of july. _____

**7.** Labor Day is in september. _____

**8.** Fire Prevention Week is during october. _____

**9.** Thanksgiving Day is in november. _____

© Great Source. All rights reserved.

**B** Unscramble these months and write them correctly on the lines below. Remember to use a capital letter for the first letter!

1. uejn  _____June_____

2. gsatuu  _____

3. hamrc  _____

4. yrjnuaa  _____

5. larip  _____

6. yma  _____

7. tbreoco  _____

8. eeedmbcr  _____

9. eyfbarru  _____

10. ljuy  _____

11. ervbnome  _____

12. tpbreesme  _____

© Great Source. All rights reserved.

*Name* _____

# Capital Letters for Holidays

Use **capital letters** for the names
of holidays.

↙ ↙
Father's Day      Thanksgiving Day

**A**  **Use capital letters for the holidays in these
sentences. (*Day* is part of many holiday names.)**

      N    Y    D

**1.** new year's day is in January.

**2.** We made cards for valentine's day.

**3.** We celebrate presidents' day in February.

**4.** mother's day and memorial day are always in May.

**5.** One holiday in June is flag day.

**6.** July 4 is independence day.

**7.** The first Monday in September is labor day.

**8.** The second Monday in October is columbus day.

© Great Source.  All rights reserved.

50

**B** Write the names of three holidays found in the sentences on page 47.

1. _____

2. _____

3. _____

Now use the names of those three holidays in sentences.

1. _____

_____

_____

2. _____

_____

_____

3. _____

_____

_____

© Great Source. All rights reserved.

Name _____

# Capital Letters
# for Names of Places

Use a **capital letter** for the name
of a city, a state, or a country.

| **City** | **State** | **Country** |
|---|---|---|
| Carson City | Nevada | France |
| Rome | Iowa | Chad |

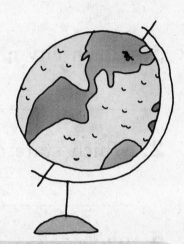

 **Write the city, state, or country correctly in the following sentences.**

**1.** *Make Way for Ducklings* takes place in the city of

boston. _____Boston_____

**2.** The Everglades are in florida. _____

**3.** My grandma is from ireland. _____

**4.** Mt. Fuji is in japan. _____

**5.** The Sears Tower is in chicago. _____

**6.** The Peach State is georgia. _____

**7.** The capital of Alaska is juneau. _____

© Great Source. All rights reserved.     previous edition page 398

**B** **Write the answers to the following questions. Use correct capitalization.**

**1.** Which city or town do you live in?

_____

**2.** Which state do you live in?

_____

**3.** What is one state that is near your home state?

_____

**4.** What city does the President of the United States live in?

_____

**5.** What country were you born in?

_____

**6.** Which country would you most like to visit?

_____

© Great Source. All rights reserved.

*Name* _____

# Capital Letter for *I*

Use a **capital letter** for the word *I*.

 I have curly red hair.
Cory and I like to tap-dance.

**A** Write the word *I* in each of these sentences.

**1.** Jimmy and ___I___ are friends.

**2.** Sometimes _____ go to his house.

**3.** _____ ride there on my bike.

**4.** Sometimes Jimmy and _____ play at the park.

**B** Write two sentences of your own using the word *I*.

**1.** _____

_____

**2.** _____

_____

© Great Source. All rights reserved.

**Draw a picture of yourself in the box below. Then write three sentences about yourself. Use the word *I* in each sentence.**

1. _____

   _____

2. _____

   _____

3. _____

   _____

© Great Source. All rights reserved.

Name _____

# Capital Letters to Begin Sentences

Always use a **capital letter** for the first word in a sentence.

**W**e go to the park in the summer.

**A** Begin each of the following sentences with a capital letter.

O

1. ȯne day we had a picnic.

2. aunt Jill brought a big bowl of fruit salad.

3. grandma made lemonade and biscuits.

4. we had sub sandwiches and carrot sticks.

5. all the kids played softball before lunch.

6. after the game everyone drank lemonade.

7. grandma's biscuits were the best part of the picnic.

8. the ants liked the crumbs we dropped.

© Great Source. All rights reserved.

**B** Put a capital letter at the beginning of each sentence. Put a period at the end of each sentence.

there's a swimming pool at our park sometimes we go there for a swim i learned how to swim last year now I can go in the deep end of the pool my little sister can't swim yet she stays in the shallow end maybe I'll teach her how to swim

Write two sentences about things you like to do in the summer. Remember to use capital letters and periods.

1. _____

_____

2. _____

_____

3. _____

_____

© Great Source. All rights reserved.

*Name*

# Capital Letter for a Speaker's First Word

Use a **capital letter** for a speaker's first word.

He asked, "Can you guess what this is?"

 **A** **Add capital letters where they are needed.**

**1.** Our teacher asked, "do you know the story of the blind
D

men and the elephant?"

**2.** "i do," said Jasmine. "one man feels the elephant's

trunk. he thinks an elephant is like a big snake."

**3.** "another man feels the ear," Kerry added. "he thinks

an elephant is like a big fan."

**4.** Jasmine said, "another man feels the leg. he thinks an

elephant is like a tree trunk."

**5.** Then Ms. Tyler asked, "how could they know the truth?"

**6.** Kerry said, "they could work and talk together."

© Great Source. All rights reserved.

58

 **B**    **Add capital letters where they are needed.**

1. Ms. Tyler said, "that's right, Kerry."

2. She asked, "when do you like to work together?"

3. Kerry answered, "i like working together to perform

   plays."

4. Jasmine added, "that's something one person can't

   usually do alone."

 **Complete this sentence telling what the elephant thinks about the blind men.**

The elephant said, "_____

_____."

© Great Source. All rights reserved.

*Name*

# Capital Letters for Book Titles

Most words in book titles begin with **capital letters.**

➤ Town Mouse, Country Mouse

Some words do not begin with capital letters (unless they are the first or last word of a title). Here are some examples:

a   an   the   and   but   of

to   with   by   for   on

 **Write the four underlined book titles correctly on the lines below.**

I went to the library yesterday. I found some wonderful books! I checked out <u>madison in new york</u>, <u>fishing with dad</u>, <u>hattie and the fox</u>, and <u>my brother needs a boa</u>.

1. <u>Madison in New York</u>

2. _____

3. _____

4. _____

© Great Source. All rights reserved.

60

**B** Write down the titles of your favorite book and magazine.

Book: _____

Magazine: _____

 Write a note telling someone about your favorite book or magazine.

Dear _____ ,

_____

_____

_____

_____

_____

Your friend,

_____

© Great Source. All rights reserved.

Name _____

# Capital Letters Review

This activity reviews some of the different ways to use **capital letters**.

 **A** **Put capital letters where they are needed. (There are 19 in all.) Watch for these things:**
* **first word in a sentence,**
* **names and titles of people, and**
* **names of cities, states, and countries.**

our class is studying rivers.  mr. banks read a

book to us about the nashua river.  the book was

written by lynne cherry.  we also learned about the

nile river in africa.  it is the longest river in the

world.  ms. johnson visited our class.  she went

down the amazon river on a raft!  she showed

slides of her trip.

© Great Source. All rights reserved.

**B** Put capital letters where they are needed.
(There are 11 in all.) Watch for:
* a speaker's first word.
* names of days and months.
* names of holidays.

**1.** Joel said, "my favorite day is sunday. What's yours?"

**2.** "sunday is my favorite day, too," I answered.

**3.** "what's your favorite month?" Molly asked.

**4.** I said, "my favorite month is july, because it's summer, and that's when I was born."

**5.** Molly said, "my favorite month is december, because that's when we celebrate hanukkah."

**6.** "that's when we celebrate christmas," I said.

**C** Put capital letters where they are needed in these titles.

**1.** the tigger movie

**2.** the fox and the hound

© Great Source. All rights reserved.

Name _____

# Plurals

**Plural** means more than one. For most nouns, make the plurals by adding **-s**.

desk ➜ desk**s**  window ➜ window**s**

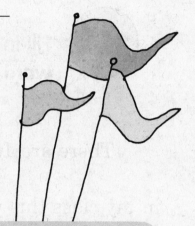

**A** Here is a list of things that may be in your classroom. Write the plural forms of the nouns. Then add two of your own examples.

**1.** flag            flags

**2.** table         _____

**3.** eraser       _____

**4.** pencil        _____

**5.** book          _____

**6.** marker      _____

**7.** door          _____

**8.** ruler          _____

**9.** _____ _____

**10.** _____ _____

© Great Source. All rights reserved.

**B** Fill in the blanks by changing the singular word under the line into a plural word.

There are 16 _____ and 10 _____
                      *(girl)*                                          *(boy)*

in my class this year. We have one teacher and two

_____ . There are three learning
*(helper)*

_____ in the classroom. In the reading center
*(center)*

there are lots of _____ . The art center has
                            *(magazine)*

some very bright _____ . In the writing center
                    *(marker)*

there's a whole box of _____ and many different
                          *(pencil)*

_____ of paper. I love my classroom!
*(kind)*

Write a sentence telling how many boys and girls there are in your class.

_____

_____

_____

© Great Source. All rights reserved.

*Name*
_____

# Plurals Using
## -s and -es 1

For most nouns, make the **plurals** by
adding **-s**.

one bird      two bird**s**
a bike      four bike**s**

For some nouns, you need to do more.
Add **-es** to words that end in **sh, ch, s,** or **x**.

a bush      some bush**es**
one box      two box**es**

 **A**    **Write the plurals of the following nouns. It's easy—just add -s.**

**1.** bug    bugs

**6.** dog _____

**2.** river _____

**7.** house _____

**3.** eye _____

**8.** desk _____

**4.** ear _____

**9.** tree _____

**5.** sister _____

**10.** lake _____

© Great Source. All rights reserved.

**Make the following nouns plural. They all end in *sh*, *ch*, *s*, or *x*. You will need to add *-es*.**

**1.** brush _____     **5.** crash _____

**2.** class _____     **6.** patch _____

**3.** bench _____     **7.** boss _____

**4.** fax _____     **8.** bunch _____

**C** **Fill in each blank with the correct plural. You will need to add *-s* to some nouns and *-es* to other nouns.**

**1.** At the petting zoo there are baby _____
(lion)

and _____ .
(fox)

**2.** There are three _____ and
(hamster)

two _____ in my classroom.
(gerbil)

**3.** My mom makes _____ for me and
(lunch)

my two _____ .
(brother)

© Great Source.  All rights reserved.

Name _____

# Plurals Using -*s* and -*es* 2

Make the **plurals** of most nouns by adding -*s*.

one snack    two snack**s**

For nouns that end in **sh**, **ch**, **s**, or **x**, add -*es* to make the plurals.

one lunch    two lunch**es**

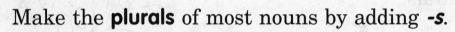

**A** Write the plurals of the following nouns. Add -*s* or -*es*.

1. apple ___apples___

2. carrot _____

3. dish _____

4. glass _____

5. spoon _____

6. box _____

7. peach _____

8. sandwich _____

9. raisin _____

10. fork _____

Draw a lunchbox on your own paper. Include some of the things you just listed.

© Great Source. All rights reserved.

# Words That Change to Make Plurals

A few nouns make their **plurals** by changing letters and words.  Here are some examples of irregular plurals.

child – children
foot – feet
goose – geese
man – men

mouse – mice
wife – wives
woman – women
wolf – wolves

**A**  **Fill in each blank with the correct plural from the nouns above.**

1. There's a song about three blind _____mice_____ .

2. You clap with your hands and walk with your _____ .

3. Ducks and _____ like to swim in ponds.

4. Sheep need to be protected from _____ .

5. Cartoons are for _____, but_____

   and _____ watch them, too.

6. Husbands have _____ .

© Great Source.  All rights reserved.

Name _____

# Plurals of Words That End in *y* 1

Here are two rules for making **plurals** of nouns ending in *y*.

**Rule 1**   If there is a consonant right before the *y*, change the *y* to *i* and add *-es*.

one ba**by**      two bab**ies**

**Rule 2**   If there is a vowel right before the *y*, just add *-s*.

one turk**ey** → three turkey**s**

**A**   **Write the plurals of the following nouns.
Use rule 1.**

**1.** cherry _____

**2.** kitty _____

**3.** party _____

**4.** berry _____

**5.** guppy _____

**6.** bunny _____

**7.** pony _____

**8.** puppy _____

**9.** country _____

**10.** worry _____

© Great Source. All rights reserved.

70

**B** Make the following nouns plural. Use rule 2 from page 69.

**1.** monkey _____     **3.** toy _____

**2.** ray _____     **4.** holiday _____

Circle three of the plurals you made on pages 69–70.  Use each one in a sentence.

**1.** _____

_____

**2.** _____

_____

**3.** _____

_____

© Great Source.  All rights reserved.

*Name* _____

# Plurals of Words That End in *y* 2

Here are two rules for making **plurals** of nouns ending in *y*.

**Rule 1**  If there is a consonant right before the *y*, change the *y* to *i* and add *-es*.

one ba**b**y    two bab**ies** ↖

**Rule 2**  If there is a vowel right before the *y*, just add *-s*.

one turk**e**y    three turkey**s** ↖

**A**  **Make the following nouns plural using rule 1 or rule 2.**

**1.** story    _____stories_____

**2.** diary    _____

**3.** donkey   _____

**4.** key      _____

**5.** baby     _____

**6.** day      _____

© Great Source. All rights reserved.

**Write Source** pages **329–331, 422,** and **424**

# Plurals Review

This activity reviews making **plurals**.

**A** Make these nouns plural by adding -s or -es.

1. glass _____       4. bus _____

2. brush _____       5. dress _____

3. frog _____        6. worm _____

**B** Make these nouns plural by adding -s or changing y to i and adding -es.

1. monkey _____      4. turkey _____

2. puppy _____       5. toy _____

3. day _____         6. cherry _____

**C** Change these words to make them plural.

1. mouse _____       3. woman _____

2. foot _____        4. knife _____

    © Great Source. All rights reserved.

Name _____

# Abbreviations

Put a **period** after a person's title.

**Mr. Mrs. Ms. Dr.**

Ms • Walters          Mr • Johnson

**A** Put periods after the people's titles in these sentences.

**1.** Mr⊙Forest is our next-door neighbor.

**2.** Mr and Mrs Forest have a very big garden.

**3.** Mrs Forest works in her garden on cool mornings.

**4.** Her friend Dr Maynard stops to visit before work.

**5.** Mrs Forest gives Dr Maynard some pretty flowers
to take to the office.

**6.** After dinner, Mr Forest likes to weed the garden.

**7.** Mrs Forest helps him water the plants.

© Great Source. All rights reserved.

**B** Think of four people who work in your school.
Write their names below.  Be sure to write Mr.,
Mrs., Ms., or Dr. before each.

1. _____

2. _____

3. _____

4. _____

KEEP GOING

Choose two of the people.
Write a sentence about each person.

1. _____

_____

2. _____

_____

© Great Source.  All rights reserved.

Name _____

# Abbreviations for Days and Months

When writing sentences, you should write the full names of the days and the months.

Today is **Tuesday**, **October 9**.

You should also know the **abbreviations** for the names of the days and the months.

Tuesday ➜ **Tues.**     October ➜ **Oct.**

**A**   Write the abbreviations for the days and months in the following lists.

**1.** Sunday      _Sun._      **7.** February   _____

**2.** Friday      _____      **8.** March      _____

**3.** Wednesday   _____      **9.** November   _____

**4.** Thursday    _____      **10.** August     _____

**5.** Saturday    _____      **11.** September  _____

**6.** Monday      _____      **12.** January    _____

© Great Source. All rights reserved.

# Post Office Abbreviations

The US Postal Service suggests using
all capital letters and no periods in
abbreviations.

948 **N** LINCOLN
**North**

 **A**   **Read the addresses below.  Write the words
for the underlined abbreviations.**

**1.** 1060 W ADDISON <u>ST</u>

Street
_____

**2.** 1600 PENNSYLVANIA <u>AVE</u>

_____

**3.** 28 <u>E</u> 20TH ST

_____

**4.** 7400 GRANT <u>RD</u>

_____

**5.** 413 <u>S</u> EIGHTH STREET

_____

**6.** 40 PRESIDENTIAL <u>DR</u>

_____

© Great Source.  All rights reserved.

*Name* _____

# Checking Mechanics Review 1

This activity reviews some of the ways to use capital letters.

 **A** **Put capital letters where they are needed. There are 21 for you to find.**

dear  theresa,

how  are  you?  how  is  life  in  florida?  today  ms. martinez  said  she  wished  we  could  all  visit  you.  i told  her  i  get  to  visit  you  in  june!

i  just  read  a  book  called  <u>lon  po  po</u>.  it  is  a good  story  from  china.  lee  gave  me  the  book  for  my birthday.

mrs.  james  said  she  hopes  you  like  your  new school.  do  you?

Your  friend,

Roger

© Great Source. All rights reserved.

**B** Fill in the blanks below. Use your *Write Source* if you need help.

**1.** Write two days of the week that are school days:

   _____      _____

**2.** Write the name of a holiday: _____

**3.** Write your first name: _____

**4.** Write the name of a planet: _____

**5.** Write your teacher's name: _____

KEEP GOING

Now use the words you just wrote to complete this story.

It was _____ , but there was no school. It
        *(day of the week)*

was _____ . _____ had a busy
      *(name of the holiday)*        *(teacher's name)*

day planned. _____ was going to build a
              *(your name)*

spaceship and blast off to _____ .
                            *(planet)*

© Great Source. All rights reserved.

*Name*

# Checking Mechanics Review 2

This activity reviews plurals and abbreviations.

 **Write the plural of each animal name.**

**1.** cow _____        **6.** mouse _____

**2.** donkey _____        **7.** fox _____

**3.** finch _____        **8.** pig _____

**4.** goose _____        **9.** puppy _____

**5.** guppy _____        **10.** turkey _____

 **Write the abbreviation for each day of the week.**

**1.** Monday _____        **5.** Friday _____

**2.** Tuesday _____        **6.** Saturday _____

**3.** Wednesday _____        **7.** Sunday _____

**4.** Thursday _____

© Great Source. All rights reserved.

Write the abbreviations for the months of the year. Notice some months are not abbreviated.

1. January _____

2. February _____

3. March _____

4. April _____

5. May _____

6. June _____

7. July _____

8. August _____

9. September _____

10. October _____

11. November _____

12. December _____

© Great Source. All rights reserved.

Name _____

# Using the Right Word 1

Some words sound alike, but they have different spellings. They also have different meanings. These words are **homophones**. Here are two examples:

My bare hands are cold.

I saw a bear at the zoo.

**A** **Fill in each blank with *bare* or *bear*.**

**1.** The panda ____bear____ lives in China.

**2.** Our teacher puts a rug on the _____ floor.

**3.** This morning I found a picture of a koala _____ .

**4.** Bees stung the boy's _____ legs.

**5.** The sun felt warm on my _____ arms.

**B** **Write a sentence using *bare* and *bear*.**

_____

_____

© Great Source. All rights reserved.

82

 **Fill in each blank with *ate* or *eight* or *ant* or *aunt*.**

*Suzzie* **ate** *two carrots today.*
*Spiders have* **eight** *legs.*

*I watched an* **ant** *crawl up the wall.*
*My* **aunt** *lives across town.*

**1.** Last year my _____ visited friends in California.

**2.** A carpenter _____ loves to eat wood.

**3.** I counted _____ sparrows sitting on the ground.

**4.** An _____ can walk on the ceiling.

**5.** I can pick up _____ rocks with one hand.

**6.** For lunch, I _____ a cheese sandwich.

**7.** Sarai's _____ _____ a tasty apple.

**D** **Write a sentence using *ate* and *eight*.**

_____

_____

© Great Source. All rights reserved.

Name

_____

# Using the Right Word 2

Some words sound alike, but they have different spellings. They also have different meanings. These words are **homophones**. Here are two examples:

The **deer** eat acorns. My aunt is **dear** to me.

**A** **Fill in each blank with *blew* or *blue*.**

The wind **blew** all day.
Some houses are painted **blue**.

**1.** Is _____blue_____ the color of the sky?

**2.** Please pick up a _____ worksheet today.

**3.** That girl just _____ a huge bubble.

**4.** Will you put this book on the _____ shelf?

**5.** The sign just _____ over.

**B** **Write a sentence using *dear* and *deer*.**

_____

_____

© Great Source. All rights reserved.

84

**Fill in each blank with *by* or *buy.***

Your pencil is **by** the dictionary.
I want to **buy** a notebook.

**1.** Can you _____ a bicycle for ten cents?

**2.** My best friend is waiting _____ the oak

tree in the park.

**3.** Will wants to _____ a birthday present

for Samuel.

**4.** The book _____ the teacher's desk

belongs to Maria.

**5.** Go stand _____ the school bus.

**D**  **Write a sentence using *for* and *four.***

_____

_____

© Great Source. All rights reserved.

Name _____

# Using the Right Word 3

Some words sound alike, but they have different spellings. They also have different meanings. These words are **homophones**. Here are some examples:

I hear you.     I am here.

 **Fill in each blank with *here* or *hear*.**

**1.** I asked my dog Dan to come _____here_____ .

**2.** Can you _____ what I am saying?

**3.** Did you _____ what happened to Sara?

**4.** _____ is the ball I thought I lost.

 **Fill in each blank with *no* or *know*.**

Anna said, **"No,** I didn't **know** that."

**1.** There is _____ more soup.

**2.** I _____ where to get some.

**3.** Just answer yes or _____ .

**4.** Do you _____ the new girl?

© Great Source. All rights reserved.

## C   Fill in each blank with *new* or *knew*.

These shoes are **new**.      I **knew** the answer.

**1.** I got a _____new_____ raincoat.

**2.** My mom _____ it was going to rain today.

**3.** Mike said he _____ how it would end.

**4.** My sister got _____ boots.

## D   Fill in each blank with *its* or *it's*.

**It's** washing **its** kitten.

**1.** The cat uses _____ tongue.

**2.** _____ washing the kitten's fur.

**3.** The kitten needs _____ mother.

**4.** _____ fun to watch the kitten grow.

## E   Write a sentence using *its* and *it's*.

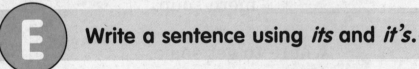

_____

_____

© Great Source. All rights reserved.

Name _____

# Using the Right Word 4

Some words sound alike, but they have different spellings. They also have different meanings. These words are **homophones**. Here are some examples:

I have two cats.
I have a dog, too.
I go to Pine Elementary.

 **A** **Fill in each blank with** *two*, *to*, **or** *too*. ***Too*** **can mean "also" or "more than enough."**

**1.** We are going _____to_____ the beach.

**2.** We can only stay for _____ hours.

**3.** Can Marla come, _____?

**4.** I like to take a radio _____ the beach.

**5.** Just don't play it _____ loud.

 **B** **Write a sentence using** *two* **and** *to*.

_____

_____

© Great Source. All rights reserved.

88

**C**    **Fill in each blank with *one* or *won*.**

**One** summer I **won** a ribbon.

1. There was _____ race.

2. I was so fast, I _____.

3. Mr. Wang gave me _____ blue ribbon.

4. I showed it to _____ of my cousins.

5. My mom couldn't believe I _____.

**D**    **Fill in each blank with *their*, *there*, or *they're*.**

We saw **their** new puppy. (*Their* shows ownership.)

**There** are three pets now.

**They're** lots of fun. (*They're* = they are.)

1. _____There_____ are four kids in the Clark family.

2. We play freeze tag in _____ backyard.

3. _____ my next-door neighbors.

4. I went to school _____ for one year.

© Great Source. All rights reserved.

Name _____

# Using the Right Word Review 1

This activity reviews the **homophones** you have practiced.

 **Write the correct word in each blank.**

**1.** Sam took _____†wo_____ rats _____ school.
      (two, to, too)                    (two, to, too)

**2.** The white rat _____ all of _____ food.
      (eight, ate)                    (its, it's)

**3.** Someone yelled, "Don't bring them in _____!"
      (hear, here)

**4.** "I don't like _____ _____ tails!"
      (they're, their, there)  (bear, bare)

**5.** Miss Green said, "I _____ what to do."
      (no, know)

**6.** "We'll get a box _____ the rats to sleep in."
      (for, four)

**7.** Other students have pets _____.
      (two, to, too)

© Great Source. All rights reserved.

**8.** Don has a _____ pet parrot.
*(new, knew)*

**9.** _____ are more than 300 kinds of parrots.
*(Their, There, They're)*

**10.** Don will _____ a book about parrots.
*(buy, by)*

**11.** Then he will _____ how to care for his pet.
*(no, know)*

**12.** You should _____ the parrot talk!
*(hear, here)*

**B** Write three sentences. Use one of these words in each sentence: *to, two, too.*

**1.** _____

_____

**2.** _____

_____

**3.** _____

_____

© Great Source. All rights reserved.

*Name* _____

# Using the Right Word Review 2

 **Before each sentence is a group of words. Choose the correct word to fill in each blank.**

1. **(hear, here)** "Did you _____ that Uncle Andy and Aunt Sue are coming _____ ?" I asked.

2. **(know, no)** "Well, _____ , I didn't _____ that," Lea answered.

3. **(Ant, Aunt)** _____ Sue got a sailboat," I said. "She painted a red _____ on the side of the boat."

4. **(their, there, they're)** "I hope _____ bringing _____ boat when they come," Lea said.

5. **(knew, new)** "Sure," I said. "They _____ we'd want to sail in the _____ boat."

© Great Source. All rights reserved.

**B** Below are three homophone pairs. Pick one pair, and draw a picture showing those words. (Use *Write Source* if you need to check meanings.) Then write a sentence about your picture.

one won    blew blue    dear deer

# Sentence Activities

This section includes activities related to basic sentence writing, kinds of sentences, and sentence problems. In addition, KEEP GOING, which is at the end of many activities, encourages follow-up practice of certain skills.

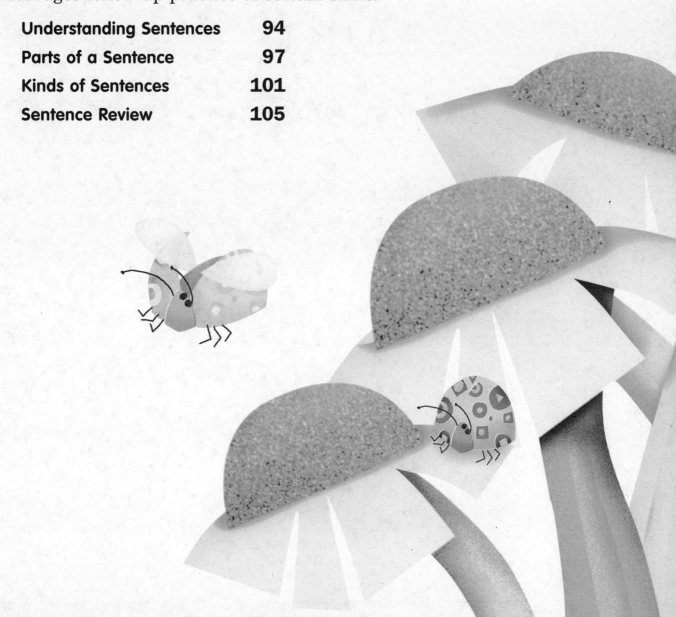

Name _____

# Understanding Sentences

A **sentence** tells a complete thought.

This is not a complete thought:
On the window.

This is a complete thought:
A bug is on the window.

 Check whether each group of words is a complete thought or not.

|  | Complete Thought | |
|---|:---:|:---:|
|  | Yes | No |
| **1.** From the downstairs music room. | _____ | ✓ |
| **2.** The sound was very loud. | _____ | _____ |
| **3.** Covered his ears. | _____ | _____ |
| **4.** After that. | _____ | _____ |
| **5.** He shut the front door. | _____ | _____ |
| **6.** Max played the drums. | _____ | _____ |
| **7.** Ming played the piano. | _____ | _____ |
| **8.** Mom the silver flute. | _____ | _____ |

© Great Source. All rights reserved.

**B** Fill in each blank with a word that completes the thought.

1. _____ was playing with a ball.

2. The _____ rolled down the hill.

3. _____ ran after it.

4. Then a big, hairy _____ ran after it, too.

5. The _____ got the ball and kept running.

6. Was the _____ gone for good?

Draw a picture about sentence 4.

© Great Source. All rights reserved.

Name _____

# Parts of a Sentence 1

Every **sentence** has two parts, the **subject** and the **predicate**. The subject is the naming part. The predicate tells what the subject is doing. It always includes the verb.

Joe **planted a seed.**

subject ↗        ↖ predicate

The dirt **covered the seed.**

subject ↗              ↖ predicate

**(A)** **Underline the subject with one line. Underline the predicate with two lines.**

**1.** Joe watered his seed every day.

**2.** He watched it carefully.

**3.** A leaf popped out.

**4.** The leaf grew larger.

**5.** A flower bloomed one morning.

**6.** Joe told his mom.

© Great Source. All rights reserved.

98

**Write a verb for each sentence.**

**1.** Mom _____ bread.

**2.** I _____ her.

**3.** I _____ the flour.

**4.** I _____ the bowls.

**5.** Mom _____ the bread in the oven.

**6.** I always _____ the first slice of bread.

**C** **Check whether the underlined words are the subject or the predicate of the sentence.**

|  | Subject | Predicate |
|---|---|---|
| **1.** Your body <u>has a lot of bones.</u> | _____ | ✔ |
| **2.** <u>Your longest bone</u> is in your leg. | _____ | _____ |
| **3.** Your ribs <u>look like a cage.</u> | _____ | _____ |
| **4.** Your smallest bone <u>is in your ear.</u> | _____ | _____ |
| **5.** <u>Jellyfish</u> have no bones. | _____ | _____ |
| **6.** <u>A skeleton</u> is all bones. | _____ | _____ |

© Great Source. All rights reserved.

*Name* _____

# Parts of a Sentence 2

Every **sentence** has two parts, the **subject** and the **predicate**. The subject is the naming part. The predicate tells what the subject is doing. It always includes the verb.

<u>Haley</u> <u>came to the party.</u>

subject ↗     ↖ predicate

**A** Fill in each blank with a word from the box. You may use some words more than once. These words are the subjects in your sentences.

| Poems | Ms. Day | Sam | Tacos |
|-------|---------|-------|-------|
| Eddy | Winter | Roses | Sarah |

**1.** _____ plays on the soccer team.

**2.** Last summer, _____ drove to Ohio.

**3.** _____ grow in Grandpa's garden.

**4.** _____ are my favorite food.

**5.** _____ sleeps in a tent.

© Great Source. All rights reserved.

**B** Fill in each blank with a verb from the box. You will use each word only once. Each verb will be included in the predicate part of the sentence.

| | | | |
|---|---|---|---|
| learned | barked | is | went |
| hit | sang | eats | gave |

**1.** Bobby _____ a home run.

**2.** The dog _____ loudly.

**3.** Steve _____ toast every morning.

**4.** Our teacher _____ us a test.

**5.** Kerry _____ a song for the class.

**6.** At camp, Cheri _____ to ride a horse.

**7.** My sister's name _____ Gail.

**8.** We all _____ for a hike yesterday.

© Great Source. All rights reserved.

Name _____

# Kinds of Sentences 1

A **telling sentence** makes a statement.
Put a period after a telling sentence.
Buster is out in the rain.

An **asking sentence** asks a question. Put
a question mark after an asking sentence.
Where is Buster?

 Write *T* before each telling sentence, and put
a period after it. Write *A* before each asking
sentence, and put a question mark after it.

___A___ **1.** What is Sandy doing?

_____ **2.** Sandy is making a bird feeder

_____ **3.** Why is she doing that

_____ **4.** She wants to see what kinds of birds will come

_____ **5.** Where will she put the bird feeder

_____ **6.** She's going to hang it in a tree

_____ **7.** What kind of food will she put in it

_____ **8.** Sandy bought some birdseed for her feeder

© Great Source. All rights reserved.

102

**B** Draw a picture of some birds at a bird feeder.

 **KEEP GOING**  Write one telling sentence and one asking sentence about your picture.

**1.** Telling Sentence:_____

_____

_____

**2.** Asking Sentence:_____

_____

_____

© Great Source. All rights reserved.

Name _____

# Kinds of Sentences 2

A **telling sentence** makes a statement.
Put a period after a telling sentence.
I'll feed Buster.

An **asking sentence** asks a question. Put
a question mark after an asking sentence.
Would you feed Buster, please?

 Write a telling sentence that is an answer for each asking sentence. Make sure you write complete sentences.

**1.** What happened to your shoes?

_____

**2.** Who left the door open?

_____

**3.** How did you get all muddy?

_____

**4.** Have you read Too Many Tamales?

_____

© Great Source. All rights reserved.

**B** Pretend that you are only four years old. Write some asking sentences that a four-year-old might ask. Two examples have been done for you.

1. Where do bugs come from?

2. Why does it get dark at night?

3. _____

4. _____

5. _____

Pick two questions from above. Write telling sentences to answer them. (Write interesting answers that are complete sentences!)

1. _____

_____

2. _____

_____

© Great Source. All rights reserved.

Name _____

# Sentence Review

This reviews what you have learned about sentences.

**Write _S_ after each sentence. Write _X_ after each group of words that is not a sentence.**

**1.** My dad and I. _____

**2.** Went to Blue Hills Park. _____

**3.** We hiked to the top of a big hill. _____

**4.** Above the clouds! _____

**5.** Then Treasure Cave. _____

**6.** It was scary and dark inside. _____

**7.** Later, we saw three fat raccoons. _____

**8.** We had a lot of fun. _____

**9.** Will visit the park again. _____

**Read page 350 in your _Write Source_ to see how the writer made one group of words a complete thought.**

© Great Source. All rights reserved.

**C** Underline and label the subjects and the predicates in the sentences that begin with *I*. The first sentence has been done for you.

Dear Grandma,

Guess what? $\underset{S}{\underline{I}}$ $\underset{P}{\underline{lost\ another\ tooth}}$! I bit into an apple.

I feel the new hole in my mouth now.

Mom will bring me to your house next week. I like

your yard. I think your new slide is great!

Will you make smoothies for me? See you soon.

Love,

John

 Copy one asking sentence and one telling sentence from the letter.

**1.** Telling Sentence:_____

_____

**2.** Asking Sentence:_____

_____

© Great Source. All rights reserved.

# Language Activities

The activities in this section are related to the parts of speech. All of the activities have a page link to *Write Source*. In addition, KEEP GOING, which is at the end of many activities, encourages follow-up practice of certain skills.

*Name* _____

# Nouns

A **noun** names a person, a place, or a thing.

| Person | Place | Thing |
|--------|-------|-------|
| student | park | pizza |
| friend | mall | candle |

 Write what each noun is: *person*, *place*, or *thing*. Add three nouns of your own.

1. firefighter     _____person_____

2. library     _____

3. hammer     _____

4. teacher     _____

5. pencil     _____

6. store     _____

7. _____

8. _____

9. _____

© Great Source. All rights reserved.

**B** Write *N* if the word is a noun. Write *X* if the word is not a noun.

_____ **1.** paper     _____ **4.** bring     _____ **7.** and

_____ **2.** go        _____ **5.** girl      _____ **8.** hot

_____ **3.** bee       _____ **6.** store     _____ **9.** kite

**C** Underline the noun in each sentence.

**1.** The bus is yellow.     **4.** Look at the duck!

**2.** The spider jumped.     **5.** The sky looks pretty.

**3.** This game is hard.     **6.** A friend called.

Write a sentence about your favorite toys. Then underline the nouns in your sentence.

_____

_____

_____

© Great Source. All rights reserved.

Name _____

# Common and Proper Nouns 1

A **common noun** names a person, place, or thing.
A **proper noun** names a special person, place, or thing.

| Common Noun | Proper Noun |
| --- | --- |
| boy | Tony Prada |
| school | Hill Elementary |
| city | Lexington |

A proper noun begins with a capital letter.
Some proper nouns are more than one word.

**A**    **Underline the common noun in each sentence.**

**1.** The <u>class</u> is busy writing.

**2.** Our teacher likes to help.

**3.** A girl is reading quietly.

**4.** The street is shiny and wet.

**5.** This sandy beach is hot.

**6.** Let's swim in the pool!

**7.** My puppy is furry and brown.

**8.** He has a red collar.

© Great Source. All rights reserved.

112

**B** Underline the proper noun in each sentence.

**1.** We stopped at Jefferson Library.

**2.** Susie wanted a book about horses.

**3.** This book is about President Lincoln.

**4.** Principal Brown visited the library.

**5.** He speaks Spanish.

**6.** Rosa Perez does, too.

**C** Write *C* if the underlined word is a common noun. Write *P* if the underlined word is a proper noun.

____ **1.** My neighbor walks her <u>dog</u> each afternoon.

____ **2.** My neighbor's name is <u>Mrs. Lee</u>.

____ **3.** Her dog likes <u>treats</u>.

____ **4.** <u>Alf</u> is a funny dog.

____ **5.** One day he got on a <u>bus</u>.

____ **6.** The bus <u>driver</u> said, "No dogs on the bus!"

© Great Source. All rights reserved.

113

Name _____

# Common and Proper Nouns 2

A **common noun** names any person, place, or thing. A **proper noun** names a special person, place, or thing.

| Common Noun | Proper Noun |
|-------------|-------------|
| holiday | New Year's Day |
| country | Mexico |

A proper noun begins with a capital letter. Some proper nouns are more than one word.

**A** Write *C* if the word is a common noun. Write *P* if the word is a proper noun.

__C__ **1.** cat       ____ **6.** Jennifer

____ **2.** Sun Park       ____ **7.** Main Street

____ **3.** library       ____ **8.** book

____ **4.** Washington, D.C.       ____ **9.** mountain

____ **5.** flag       ____ **10.** Rocky Mountains

© Great Source. All rights reserved.

114

## B

**Draw a line from each common noun to the proper noun that fits with it.**

1. girl                          United States

2. boy                          Fluffy

3. cat                          "The Three Bears"

4. country                      Tom

5. story                        Lisa

## C

**Write _C_ if the underlined noun is a common noun. Write _P_ if the underlined noun is a proper noun.**

_____ 1. Today is Christmas!

_____ 2. There is no school today.

_____ 3. The air is freezing cold.

_____ 4. Aunt Lizzie visited us.

_____ 5. Kevin brought popcorn.

_____ 6. Chin is from Korea.

© Great Source. All rights reserved.

*Name*
_____

# Singular and Plural Nouns

**Singular** means one.

elephant

**Plural** means more than one.

elephant**s**↖

Plural nouns usually end with ***s***.

**A** — **Write *S* if the noun is singular. Write *P* if the noun is plural.**

_P_ **1.** boxes          ____ **4.** rug

____ **2.** table          ____ **5.** truck

____ **3.** chairs          ____ **6.** toys

**B** — **Write *S* if the underlined noun is singular. Write *P* if the underlined noun is plural.**

____ **1.** I like <u>art</u>.          ____ **3.** <u>Paints</u> are messy.

____ **2.** I have <u>crayons</u>.          ____ **4.** It's for my <u>sister</u>.

© Great Source. All rights reserved.

## C  Underline the plural noun in each sentence.

1. The cow has black and white spots.

2. Some piglets are pink.

3. Potatoes spilled out of the grocery bag.

4. My sister baked dinner rolls yesterday.

5. Tony took off his muddy shoes.

6. Erin held the tiny kittens.

**KEEP GOING**

Draw a picture about one of the plural nouns you underlined. Write the noun under your picture.

© Great Source.  All rights reserved.

Name _____

# Possessive Nouns

A **possessive noun** shows ownership.
A possessive noun has an **apostrophe**.

Tia's toy boat was left out in the yard.
(The toy boat belongs to Tia.)

After the storm, we found it in the dog's house.
(The house belongs to the dog.)

 **Circle the possessive nouns.**

1. (Mike's) story about Mr. Bug was fun to read.

2. Mr. Bug's house was flooded when it rained.

3. Mr. Bug's family hopped in a toy boat.

4. All the little Bugs waited for the storm's end.

5. Finally, the boat floated to a dog's house.

6. The dog's name was Buddy.

7. The little Bugs asked if they could share their new

    friend's home.

8. The story's title is "The Bugs Find a Buddy."

© Great Source. All rights reserved.

**B** Draw a picture of one of these things from the story:

* Mr. Bug's flooded house.
* the child's toy boat.
* the dog's house.

Write a sentence telling about your picture. Use a possessive noun. (Remember to use an apostrophe.)

_____

_____

© Great Source. All rights reserved.

Name _____

# Pronouns 1

A **pronoun** is a word that takes the place of a noun.

| **Noun** | **Pronoun** |
|---|---|
| Todd did it. | He did it. |
| Sally laughed. | She laughed. |
| The rope broke. | It broke. |
| The skates are too big. | They are too big. |

 **Circle the pronouns that replace the underlined nouns in the sentences below.**

**1.** <u>Holly</u> gave Katy a Mexican coin.

(She) gave Katy a Mexican coin.

**2.** Katy put the <u>coin</u> in a safe place.

Katy put it in a safe place.

**3.** <u>Peggy and Jo</u> wanted to see the coin.

They wanted to see the coin.

**4.** Then <u>Jay</u> asked to see it, too.

Then he asked to see it, too.

© Great Source. All rights reserved.

**B** Draw a line from each noun to the pronoun that could replace it.

1. Dad and Mom          he

2. the girl          it

3. Grandpa          I

4. the TV          we

5. Shari and I          they

6. _____          she
(write your first name here)

**C** In each sentence, write a pronoun to replace the noun. If you need help, check the list of pronouns on page 334 in *Write Source*.

1. _____ went to a movie.
(Jim and Ray)

2. _____ broke his arm.
(The boy)

3. A doctor fixed _____ .
(the arm)

4. _____ is a good writer.
(Jane)

 © Great Source. All rights reserved.

Name _____

# Pronouns 2

A **pronoun** can take the place of a
possessive noun. A possessive noun
shows ownership.

| **Noun** | **Pronoun** |
|---|---|
| Jan's bicycle | her bicycle |
| Dave's skateboard | his skateboard |
| the **bird's** wing | its wing |
| Mike and Laura's poem | their poem |

 **Circle the pronouns that take the place of the underlined nouns in the sentences below.**

**1.** Juanita's coat is red.

(Her) coat is hanging up.

**2.** At the picnic, Jake's lunch fell into the water.

His lunch was soggy.

**3.** Yesterday Sam and Sarah missed the bus.

Their bus left early.

**4.** The dog was very excited.

It chewed on a big bone.

© Great Source. All rights reserved.

**B** Underline the pronoun in each sentence. Draw a picture of the pet rat.

1. Here is my pet rat.

2. Dad likes its pink ears.

3. Mom likes its long tail.

4. Bogart is our favorite pet.

5. He has red eyes.

6. Ted pets his white fur.

7. We bought a blue cage.

**C** Draw a line to the pronoun that could replace the underlined words.

1. I heard Tim and Judy's song.                    ours

2. I know your sister's name.                       Its

3. Here comes Ricky's friend.                       their

4. The book's cover got wet.                        his

5. The tree house is yours and mine.                her

© Great Source. All rights reserved.

Name _____

# Pronouns 3

A **pronoun** is a word that takes the place of a noun.

**Jason** made a **sandwich**.
Then **he** ate **it**.
(The pronouns *he* and *it* take the place of the nouns *Jason* and *sandwich*.)

 **Fill in each blank with a pronoun that replaces the underlined word or words.**

**1.** Joe and Ann read a poem. __They__ read it aloud.

**2.** Tanya drew a map. _____ showed it to me.

**3.** My brother and I have a clubhouse. _____ made it ourselves.

**4.** I hope you're coming to my party. _____ will be fun.

**5.** Mom heard our music. _____ was too loud.

**6.** Tony is coming over. _____ is my friend.

**7.** The monkeys ate bananas. _____ were hungry.

**8.** This book is great. _____ has good pictures, too.

© Great Source. All rights reserved.

124

 **B** Use each pronoun in a sentence.

| | | | |
|---|---|---|---|
| I | we | she | they |

1. _____

2. _____

3. _____

4. _____

 **C** Draw a picture to go with one of your sentences.

© Great Source. All rights reserved.

Name _____

# Action Verbs

There are different kinds of **verbs**.
Some verbs show action:

Mom **found** our jump rope.
She **gave** it to us.

 **A**   **Underline the action verb in each sentence.**

**1.** Al <u>brings</u> the jump rope.

**2.** Eli and Linda hold the rope.

**3.** They twirl the rope.

**4.** The other kids count.

**5.** Scott's dog barks at the children.

**6.** Today Al jumps 100 times!

**7.** Then Linda takes a turn.

**8.** Mother waves from the window.

**9.** The kids laugh.

© Great Source. All rights reserved.

126

 **B**

Here are some more action verbs. Fill in each blank with a verb from this box.

| | | |
|---|---|---|
| dive | hear | pop |
| roars | visit | eat |

**1.** Paul and Ann _____ the zoo.

**2.** They _____ some lions.

**3.** One of the lions _____ at them.

**4.** The elephants _____ lots of peanuts.

**5.** The polar bears _____ into the pool.

**6.** Prairie dogs _____ out of their tunnels.

**Write a sentence about the zoo. Use an action verb.**

_____

_____

_____

© Great Source. All rights reserved.

Name

_____

# Action and Linking Verbs

**Action verbs** show action.  Here are some examples:

kick   tell   throw   ask   run   write

**Linking verbs** complete a thought or an idea.  Here are some examples:

am   was   is   were   are   be

 **Write _A_ if the underlined verb is an action verb. Write _L_ if the verb is a linking verb.**

_A_ **1.** Soccer players <u>kick</u> the ball.

_____ **2.** Football players <u>throw</u> the ball.

_____ **3.** I <u>am</u> cold.

_____ **4.** Pat and Rob <u>run</u> around the track.

_____ **5.** She <u>is</u> a fast runner.

_____ **6.** They <u>are</u> both in second grade.

_____ **7.** He <u>paints</u> pictures.

_____ **8.** Pete and Joni <u>were</u> sick.

© Great Source.  All rights reserved.

 **B** Pick five action verbs from the list on page 464 in *Write Source*. Use each action verb in a sentence.

1. _____

_____

2. _____

_____

3. _____

_____

4. _____

_____

5. _____

_____

 Write a sentence using the linking verb *am*.

_____

 © Great Source. All rights reserved.

Name _____

# Verbs: Present and Past Tense

A verb that tells what is happening now is called a **present-tense verb**.

Sean **is** in second grade.
He **takes** swimming lessons every week.

A verb that tells what happened in the past is called a **past-tense verb**.

Last year he **was** in first grade.
He **learned** to play soccer.

 **Check whether each underlined verb is in the present tense or the past tense.**

| | Present Tense | Past Tense |
|---|---|---|
| **1.** Bobby <u>broke</u> his leg last weekend. | _____ | ✓ |
| **2.** He <u>fell</u> out of a big tree. | _____ | _____ |
| **3.** Now he <u>has</u> a cast on his leg. | _____ | _____ |
| **4.** He <u>is</u> home from school this week. | _____ | _____ |
| **5.** Yesterday I <u>took</u> him his homework. | _____ | _____ |
| **6.** I <u>wrote</u> my name on his cast. | _____ | _____ |
| **7.** Bobby <u>walks</u> with crutches. | _____ | _____ |

© Great Source. All rights reserved.

130

 **Complete the following sentences. Write the present-tense verb or the past-tense verb in the blank. The first one has been done for you.**

## Present Tense

**1.** Now Mom _____makes_____ my lunches for school.
*(makes, made)*

**2.** Now I _____ eight years old.
*(am, was)*

**3.** The sidewalk _____ slippery when it snows.
*(gets, got)*

**4.** Now Stanis _____ swimming lessons.
*(takes, took)*

## Past Tense

**1.** Last week I _____ to school with Hector.
*(walk, walked)*

**2.** Yesterday Lydia _____ a letter to her aunt.
*(write, wrote)*

**3.** Last summer our family _____ camping.
*(goes, went)*

**4.** This morning I _____ late for school.
*(am, was)*

© Great Source. All rights reserved.

Name _____

# Irregular Verbs

Irregular verbs do not follow the same rules as other verbs. They change in different ways.

|  Present tense | Past tense |
| --- | --- |
| **Example:** Birds **fly**. | Birds **flew**. |

Study the irregular verbs in your textbook. Then complete the exercise below.

**A** Circle the correct verb in each sentence.

**1.** My friend Kara (*rode, ridden*) a pony.

**2.** Uncle Billy (*came, come*) to visit us.

**3.** Last night, I (*sung, sang*) with my cousin.

**4.** Alfonso (*saw, seen*) a moose at the zoo.

**5.** Oscar (*done, did*) a good job on his art project.

**6.** The pitcher (*threw, throw*) the ball to first base.

© Great Source. All rights reserved.

**In the sentences below, fill in the blank with the correct form of the verb shown.**

1. **was    am**

   present:  I _____ taking dance lessons.

   past:  I started dancing when I _____ four.

2. **hide    hid**

   present:  Sometimes, I _____ from my dog.

   past:  Yesterday, I _____ from him.

3. **ran    run**

   present:  We _____ with my big brother.

   past:  Last week, we _____ at the track.

4. **knew    know**

   present:  I _____ Olivia.

   past:  When we met, I _____ we would be friends.

© Great Source. All rights reserved.

Name _____

# Adjectives 1

An **adjective** describes a noun or a pronoun. An adjective often comes before the word it describes.

Megan has long hair.
Randy wears a black cap.

Sometimes an **adjective** comes after the word it describes.

Parrots are colorful.

 **A** **Underline the adjective that describes each circled noun.**

**1.** Elephants are <u>huge</u> (animals.)

**2.** Their (skin) is wrinkled.

**3.** Their ivory (tusks) are long (teeth.)

**4.** Elephants use their floppy (ears) as giant (fans.)

**5.** An elephant's trunk works as a useful (tool.)

**6.** It can pick up small (peanuts.)

**7.** A cool (river) is an elephant's favorite (place.)

© Great Source. All rights reserved.

134

**B**  **Fill in each blank with an adjective that describes the circled noun.**

**1.** Elephants make _____ (noises.)

**2.** Elephants have _____ (trunks.)

**3.** They have _____ (feet.)

**4.** Elephants can carry _____ (loads.)

**5.** Would you take a _____ (ride) on an

elephant?

**6.** How would you get on a _____ (elephant?)

**C**  **Underline each adjective that describes the circled pronoun.**

**1.** (You) are  smart.        **5.** (It) is  green.

**2.** (He) is  funny.          **6.** (We) are  cold.

**3.** (They) look  tired.       **7.** (She) feels  sick.

**4.** (I) am  hungry.          **8.** (They) taste  stale.

© Great Source.  All rights reserved.

Name _____

# Adjectives 2

An **adjective** describes a noun or a pronoun.  An adjective often comes before the word it describes.

The hungry bear sniffed the berries.

Sometimes an **adjective** comes after the word it describes.

The bear was hungry.

 **A**   **Underline the adjectives in this story. There are 14 in all. (Don't underline *a* or *that*.)**

Once there was a little brown bear.

In the cool forest, she ate crunchy roots and red berries.

She drank from a clear stream.

Fish swam by the little bear.

On summer days, the bear ate and ate.

In the fall, little bear changed.

She was a great, big bear.

She crawled into a cozy den for a long winter nap.

© Great Source. All rights reserved.

136

**B** Write one more sentence for the story about the little bear. Underline the adjectives you use.

_____

_____

**C** Write two sentences using adjectives from the box below. Try using more than one adjective in your sentences.

| | | | |
|---|---|---|---|
| hairy | purple | loud | cold |
| windy | wet | sweet | soft |
| chewy | sleepy | strong | sour |

1. _____

_____

2. _____

_____

© Great Source. All rights reserved.

*Name*
_____

# Articles

The words **a**, **an**, and ***the*** are
**articles**.

Use **a** before a consonant sound.

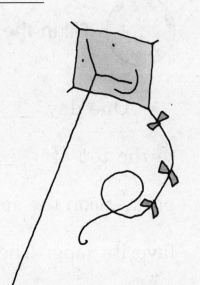

↗**a** kite

Use **an** before a vowel sound.

↗**an** ocean

**A**  **Write *a* or *an* before the following words.**

| | | |
|---|---|---|
| **an** 1. attic | | _____ 10. whale |
| _____ 2. chicken | | _____ 11. shadow |
| _____ 3. shovel | | _____ 12. envelope |
| _____ 4. elephant | | _____ 13. idea |
| _____ 5. tooth | | _____ 14. monkey |
| _____ 6. giant | | _____ 15. orange |
| _____ 7. dinosaur | | _____ 16. package |
| _____ 8. apple | | _____ 17. kettle |
| _____ 9. spider | | _____ 18. inchworm |

© Great Source. All rights reserved.

138

## B Fill in the word *a* or *an* in the spaces below.

One day _____ spider with yellow feet climbed

to the top of _____ slide. The slide was in _____

park. Soon the spider heard _____ radio playing her

favorite song. The song was _____ old tune called

"The Eensy Weensy Spider." The spider began to tap her

eight yellow feet. _____ inchworm heard the music,

too. He inched his way over to the slide and began to tap

all of his feet. What _____ funny sight to see!

_____ spider and _____ inchworm were dancing in

the park.

KEEP GOING

**Draw a picture of the spider and
the inchworm. Add a new sentence to
your picture.**

© Great Source. All rights reserved.

Name _____

# Adjectives That Compare

**Adjectives** use different word endings to make comparisons. The ending **-er** compares two people, places or things. The ending **-est** compares three or more.

Compare **two**:

My brother's room is small**er** than my room.

Compare **three or more**:

The baby's room is the small**est** room in our house.

**A** **Fill in each blank with the correct form of the adjective.**

long, longer, longest

**1.** A grass snake is ___long___.

**2.** A boa is _____ than a grass snake.

**3.** A python is the _____ snake in the zoo.

funny, funnier, funniest

**1.** Garrett's riddle was _____.

**2.** Leah's riddle was _____ than Garrett's riddle.

**3.** Ty's riddle was the _____ one in class.

© Great Source. All rights reserved.

**B** Circle the adjective that compares two people, places, or things. Underline the adjective that compares three or more.

**1.** Kenny is the tallest player on the team.

**2.** Silver Lake is deeper than Cross Creek.

**C** Write one sentence using the first adjective. Then, write another sentence using the second adjective.

bigger

_____

_____

happiest

_____

_____

© Great Source. All rights reserved.

Name _____

# Adverbs

An **adverb** is a word that describes a verb. It tells *when*, *where*, or *how* an action is done.

Some adverbs tell **when:**
yesterday    soon    always    early

Some adverbs tell **where:**
here    inside    up    below

Some adverbs tell **how:**
quietly    carefully    loudly    quickly

**A** **In each sentence below, circle the adverb that tells *when*.**

**1.** Aldo has never seen snow.

**2.** We woke up early so we could go fishing.

**3.** Tomorrow, our class is going to the museum.

**4.** Salma always wears her hair in braids.

© Great Source. All rights reserved.

142

**B** In each sentence below, fill in the blank with an adverb that tells *where*.

**1.** Our teacher will be _____ tomorrow.

**2.** Do you want to play _____ this afternoon?

**3.** I saw a mouse run _____ the stairs!

**C** Fill in each blank with an adverb from the box below. These adverb tells *how*.

| gently | quickly | softly | cheerfully |

**1.** Alexis smiled _____ when she won the race.

**2.** "Have you seen Cory?" I asked _____.

**3.** Malik danced _____ as he sang.

**4.** I rocked my baby sister _____.

© Great Source. All rights reserved.

*Name* _____

# Prepositions

A **preposition** is used to add information to a sentence.

Toby hit the ball **over** the fence.

Ally put a quarter **in** her bank.

Here are some common prepositions.

| | | | | |
|---|---|---|---|---|
| onto | up | with | at | of |
| before | below | like | in | to |
| as | over | down | along | on |

**A** Circle the prepositions in the paragraph below. The chart above will help you.

Troy left camp (before) breakfast. 2. He pushed his bike to the top of the hill. 3. Soon, he was racing down it. 4. The wind rushed through his hair. 5. The bike's wheels bumped along the grassy path. 6. "Woo-hoo!" Troy shouted with joy.

© Great Source. All rights reserved.

**B**  Use the prepositions in this box to complete the following sentences. You will use one of the prepositions twice.

| like | of | in | above | until |
|------|-----|-----|-------|-------|

**1.** Beluga whales live _____ cold, Arctic waters.

**2.** Belugas are gray _____ they become adults.

**3.** Then they turn white _____ their parents.

**4.** They are often called "sea canaries" because _____ their songs and chatter.

**5.** Belugas swim _____ groups called pods.

**6.** Their sounds can be heard _____ the water.

**C**  Write a sentence including a preposition from the box above.

_____

_____

_____

© Great Source. All rights reserved.

Name _____

# Conjunctions

A **conjunction** connects words or groups of words. The words *and* and *but* are the most common conjunctions.

Ramon writes poems **and** sings songs.

I was on time, **but** Tom wasn't there.

 **Write one sentence using the conjunction *and*.**

_____

_____

 **Write one sentence using the conjunction *but*.**

_____

_____

© Great Source. All rights reserved.

Two other conjunctions that connect words or groups of words are *or* and *so*.

Is Todd **or** Jaimee ready to bat?

It looked like rain, **so** she brought an umbrella.

 **C** **Circle the seven conjunctions in the story below.**

# The Tortoise and the Hare

Who won the race, the tortoise or the hare? They started out together, but the hare was much faster. He was way ahead of the tortoise, so he took a nap. The hare was snoring and dreaming when the tortoise walked by. Soon, the hare woke up, and he was amazed at what he saw. The tortoise was near the finish line! The hare ran to catch up, but it was too late. The tortoise won the race.

 **D** **Write a sentence using the conjunction *or*.**

_____

© Great Source. All rights reserved.

*Name*
_____

# Interjections

An **interjection** shows excitement.
Some common interjections are:

| | | |
|---|---|---|
| Wow! | Yum! | Help! |
| Ouch! | Oops! | Hey! |

 **Write interjections to complete these sentences.**

**1.** _____ ! This soup tastes delicious.

**2.** _____ ! I dropped my slice of pizza.

**3.** _____ ! I'm falling off the swing.

 **Write a sentence using one of the interjections from above.**

_____

_____

© Great Source. All rights reserved.     previous edition page 456

**C**  **Draw a picture for each sentence below. Label each picture with an interjection.**

_____
(interjection)

Look what I can do.

_____
(interjection)

That bug is huge.

_____
(interjection)

I pinched my finger!

_____
(interjection)

I dropped my lunch tray.

© Great Source. All rights reserved.

Name _____

# Parts of Speech Review 1

In this activity, you will review the parts of speech you have practiced: **noun (N)**, **pronoun (P)**, **verb (V)**, and **adjective (A)**.

 **What part of speech is underlined in each sentence? Write *N*, *P*, *V*, or *A* in the blank.**

_____ **1.** I like <u>toasted</u> cheese sandwiches.

_____ **2.** They <u>smell</u> buttery and <u>look</u> golden brown.

_____ **3.** When I <u>bite</u> into one, I <u>see</u> the melted cheese.

_____ **4.** Toasted cheese <u>sandwiches</u> taste crunchy on the outside and creamy in the middle.

_____ **5.** <u>My</u> mom makes them on the griddle.

_____ **6.** <u>I</u> could eat one every day!

_____ **7.** I hope we have toasted cheese sandwiches for <u>dinner</u> tonight.

_____ **8.** It would be a <u>super</u> way to end my day.

© Great Source. All rights reserved.

## B Fill in the blanks below.

**1.** Write the name of your favorite food (noun):

_____

**2.** Write a word that describes it (adjective):

_____

## C Fill in each blank with a word that is the correct part of speech.

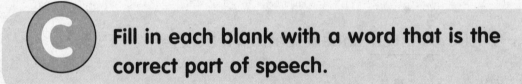

**1.** _____ likes tuna sandwiches.
      *(noun)*

**2.** _____ like tacos better.
      *(pronoun)*

**3.** I _____ two tacos every day.
      *(verb)*

**4.** I like them with _____ cheese.
                        *(adjective)*

**5.** Sandra's mom _____ the best tacos.
                    *(verb)*

**6.** She puts _____ sauce on them.
           *(adjective)*

© Great Source. All rights reserved.

*Name*
_____

# Parts of Speech Review 2

 **A** Use the adjectives and adverbs in the box below to fill in the blanks in the sentences. Use each word only once.

| | | | |
|---|---|---|---|
| small | smaller | smallest | tallest |
| exciting | large | wild | |

**1.** Our zoo is an _____ place to visit.

**2.** Many _____ animals live there.

**3.** Some are _____ and others are _____.

**4.** The giraffe is the zoo's _____ animal.

**5.** Otters and beavers are _____ animals.

**6.** Chipmunks are the _____ animals at the zoo.

© Great Source. All rights reserved.

**B** Underline the prepositions in these sentences.

**1.** One cat rested on the desktop.

**2.** Another cat hid inside a drawer.

**3.** It hid under some papers.

**C** Use a comma and a conjunction to combine these short sentences. Use *or*, *and*, or *but*.

**1.** Should we play inside? Should we play outside?

_____

**2.** We went to the park. We had a picnic.

_____

**D** Write a sentence. Use one of the interjections below.

**Wow!**     **Yippee!**     **Help!**

_____

_____

© Great Source. All rights reserved.